Yazoo Starter Pupils' Book

Hello. I'm (Cabu). What's your name?

3

1 I'm a lion.

1 Listen and point. Then say. 🔊

2 Look and listen. 🔊

3 Listen again and say. 🔊

lion, elephant, parrot, boy, girl
Hello. I'm (Trumpet). What's your name? I'm a (lion).

4 Listen and point. •))

1   2   3

5 Make a mask. Then listen and say. •))

6 Draw and say.

Hello. I'm (Cabu). I'm a (lion). What's your name?

7 Listen and point. Then say. •))

8 Look and listen. •))

9 Listen again and say. •))

banana, flower, bee, hippo
Stop! Look!

10 **Listen and circle.** •))

1

2

3

4

5

6

11 **Listen and point. Then sing.** •))

1

2

3

Look, an elephant and a bee.

7

2 It's red.

1 Listen and point. Then say. 🔊

2 Look and listen. 🔊

3 Listen again and say. 🔊

yellow, blue, red, green
It's yellow.

8

4 **Listen and stick.** •))

1

2

3

4

5 **Colour and say.**

6 **Point and say.**

Look, it's (green).

7 Listen and point. Then sing.

8 Colour and say.

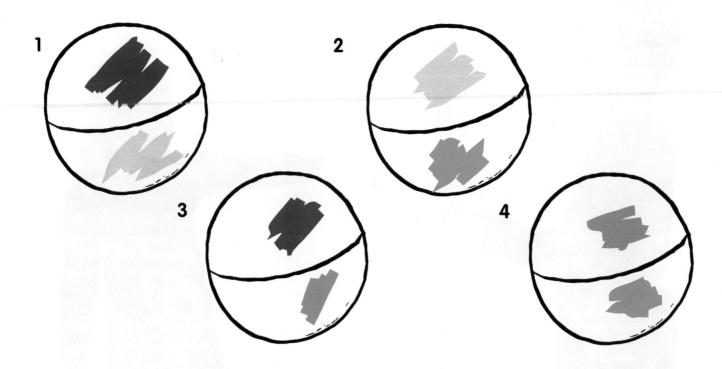

1

2

3

4

red, yellow, green, blue
It's (red) and (yellow).

9 **Listen and answer yes or no.** •))

1

2

3

4

5

10 **Play.**

banana, flower, bee, parrot
Is it yellow? Yes/No.

Playing

 Listen and point. Then say. •))

 Look and listen. •))

ball, dog
Hello. I'm sorry. Thank you.

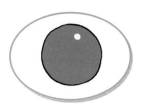

3 **Act out.**

1 **Find and tick.**

2 Listen and tick. What is it? •))

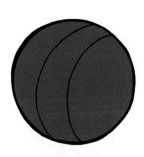

3 Make and do. Then say.

a girl, a ball, a lion
Look, it's a hippo.

15

Five bananas

1 **Listen and point. Then say.** •))

2 **Look and listen.** •))

3 **Listen again and say.** •))

one, two, three, four, five
five (bees)

4 Listen and circle. •))

5 Point and say.

6 Draw and colour. Then match.

1

2

3

4

5

7 Listen and stick. Then sing. ·))

one, two, three, four, five
five yellow bananas

8 Look and count. Then match and say.

1   2   3   4   5

9 Play.

four (parrots)

4 Here's your desk.

    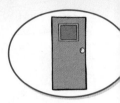

2 Look and listen. 🔊

3 Listen again and say. 🔊

teacher, desk, chair, book, door
Here's your (desk).

20

4 Listen and circle.

1 2 3

4 5

5 Point and say.

6 Play.

Here's your (chair). 21

7 **Listen and point. Then sing.** •))

 8 **Point and say.**

Here's your (desk). Here's the teacher.

9 **Find and count. Then say.**

10 **Draw and colour. Then say.**

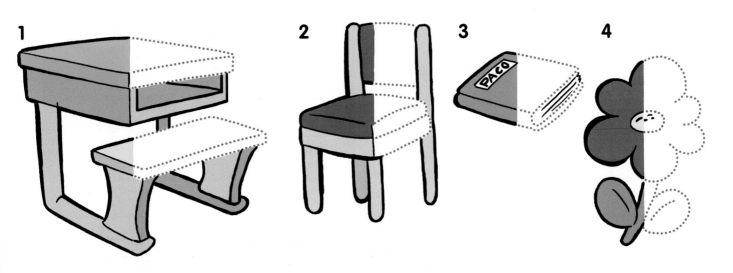

1   2   3   4

one, two, three, four, five; five (bananas)
It's a (desk). It's (green) and (yellow).

23

The green boy

 Listen and point. Then say. •)) **Look and listen.** •))

alien, apple
Look! Here's your (desk). Go to your (desk).

24

3 **Act out.**

1 Tick what changes. Then say.

2 **Stick and say.**

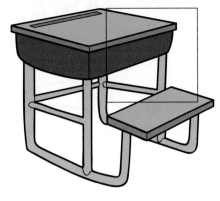

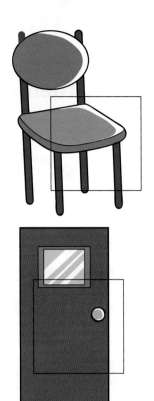

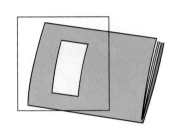

3 **Draw and make. Then say.**

5 It's a pencil.

1 Listen and point. Then say. •))

2 Look and listen. •))

3 Listen again and say. •))

bag, pencil, crayon, rubber
What is it? It's a (bag).

28

4 Listen and circle.))

1
2
3
4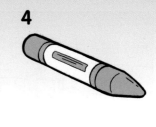

5 Point and say.

1
2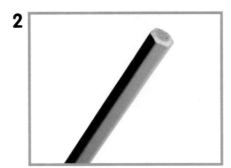
3

4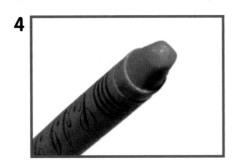
5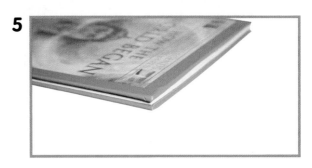

6 Ask and answer.

1
2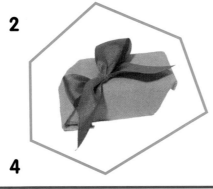
3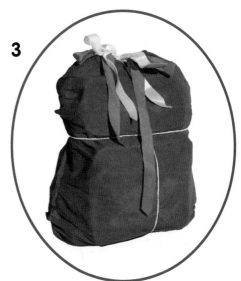
4

What is it? It's a (pencil). Yes/No.

7 Listen and stick. Then sing. •))

8 Draw and colour. Then say.

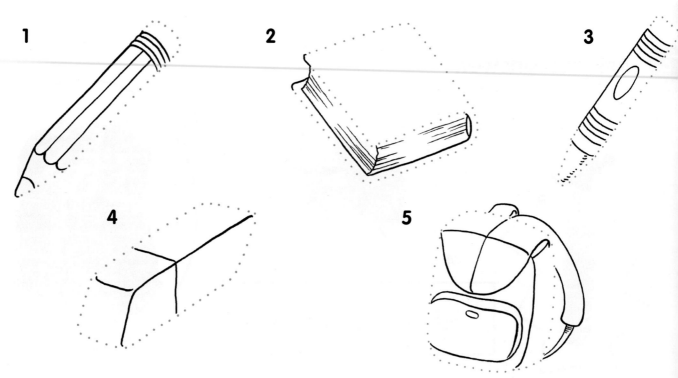

1

2

3

4

5

It's a (pencil). It's (blue).

9 **Listen and circle.** •))

1 2 3 4 5

10 **Point, ask and answer.**

11 **Play.**

Is it a (pencil)? Yes/No.

6 Stand up!

1 Listen and point. Then say. •))

2 Look and listen. •))

3 Listen again and say. •))

sit down, stand up, clap, turn around

4 Listen and number. •))

a

[ ]

b

[ ]

c

[1]

d

[ ]

5 Point and say.

6 Play.

33

7 Listen and point. Then sing.

8 Sing and do.

9 Point and say.

sit down, stand up, clap, turn around

10 **Draw and colour. Then say.**

1

2
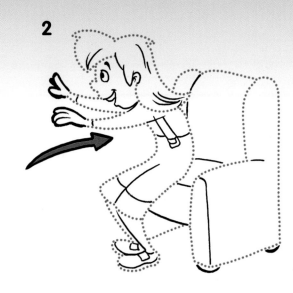

11 **Guess and say.**

12 **Listen and do.** •))

Super Ant

 Listen and point. Then say. •))

 Look and listen. •))

fish, ant
Listen! now; Well done (girls)!

3 **Act out.**

1 Follow and say. Then play.

2 **Look and draw. Then say.**

1

2

3

3 **Draw and make. Then say.**

7 This is my family.

1 Listen and point. Then say. •))

2 Look and listen. •))

3 Listen again and say. •))

mum, dad, brother, sister, me
This is my (brother).

40

4 **Listen and number.** •))

5 **Point and say.**

6 **Draw your family. Then say.**

This is my (mum).

7 **Listen and stick. Then sing.** 🔊

8 **Listen and say** yes **or** no. 🔊

1

2

3

4

This is my (mum): Hello.

9 **Find and say.**

10 **Play.**

I'm Cabu. This is my (brother). This is my family.

43

8 I've got a bike.

1 Listen and point. Then say. •))

2 Look and listen. •))

3 Listen again and say. •))

train, plane, bike, guitar
I've got a (bike) and a (guitar).

4 Listen and circle. •))

1

2

3

4

5 Point and say.

1

2

3

4

5

6

Look! I've got a (plane).

45

Listen and stick. Then sing. 🔊

7 **Listen and colour.** 🔊

1

2

3

4

(yellow) bike / train / ball / plane / guitar
I've got a (red bike).

46

8 Listen and match. •))

1   2   3   4   5

a   b   c   d   e

9 Draw and colour. Then say.

My favourite toy is my (blue bike).

At the park

1 **Listen and point. Then say.** •))   2 **Look and listen.** •))

car, kite
Be careful!; new

3 **Act out.**

Jungle Fun 4

1 **Circle the odd one out. Then say.**

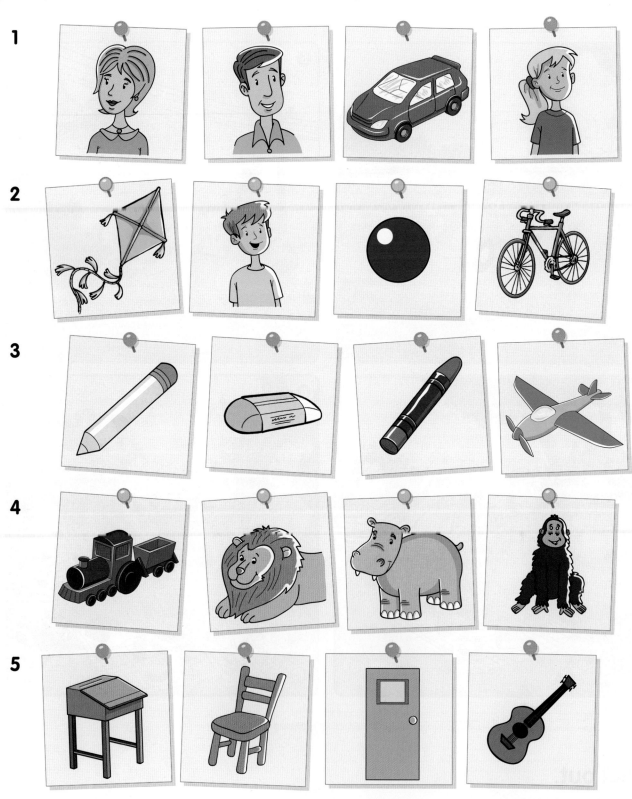

1

2

3

4

5

Listen and find. Then say. •))

1   2   3   4

3 Draw and make. Then say.

OUR TOYS

Look. This is my (ball). My favourite toy is my (train).

9 I can see a pink bird.

1 **Listen and point. Then say.**))

2 **Look and listen.**))

3 **Listen again and say.**))

pink, black, orange, white
I can see a (bird).

52

4 Listen and circle. •))

1   2   3   4

5 Point and say.

6 Draw and colour. Then say.

1   2

3   4

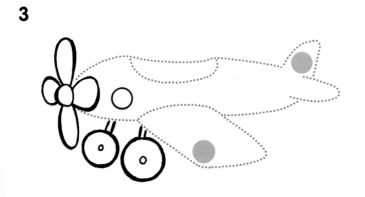

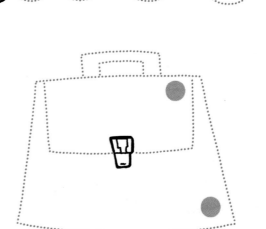

I can see (a pink bag). I can see (a black bike).   53

7 **Listen and stick. Then sing.** 🔊

8 **Say what's next. Then draw.**

a big (green ball); a small (pink ball)
I can see (two bags).

9 **Find and say.**

10 **Match and say.**

I can see (a pink bag).
I'm (Miss Maru). My favourite colour is (orange).

1 Listen and point. Then say. 🔊

2 Look and listen. 🔊

3 Listen again and say. 🔊

six, seven, eight, nine, ten (pencils)
How old are you? Happy birthday!

4 Match and say.

6

7

8

9

10

5 Count and say what's next.

1 – 3 – 5 – 7 – – 9 –

6 Guess and say.

one, two, three, four, five, six, seven, eight, nine, ten

7 **Listen and stick. Then sing.**

8 **Say and clap.**

ten, nine, eight, seven, six (red) apples

9 **Find and count. Then say.**

10 **Draw and colour.**

11 **Ask and answer.**

Look! Two fish.
How old are you? I'm (six). Happy birthday! Thank you.

Story Time 5

The balloon

1 Listen and point. Then say. •))   **2** Look and listen. •))

cake, balloon
It's nice.

3 **Act out.**

Jungle Fun 5

1 Look. Count and say.

2 Write numbers and play Bingo.

7 10
2
1 6
3
9 8
4
5

3 Draw and make. Then say.

Happy Birthday

Red seven.
I'm (8). Happy birthday.

1 Listen and point. Then say. •))

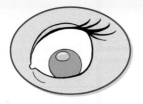   

2 Look and listen. •))

3 Listen again and say. •))

eye, nose, ear, mouth
I've got (two ears) and (a mouth).

4 Listen and number. •)))

a   b   c   d

___   1   ___   ___

5 Point and say.

6 Play.

I've got (two ears). Touch your (nose).

7 Listen and point. Then sing.

a

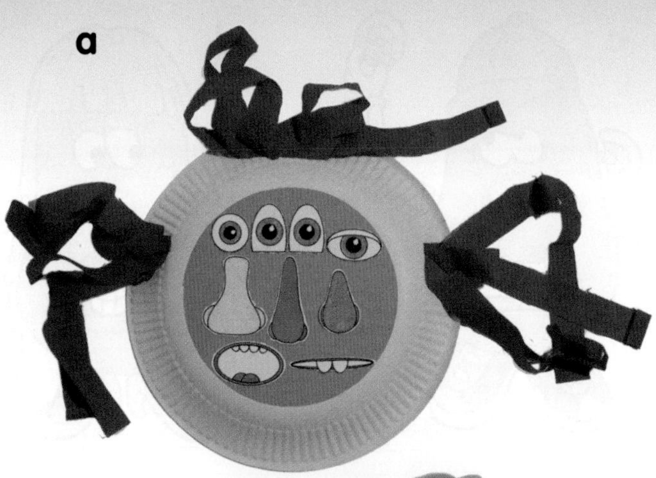

b

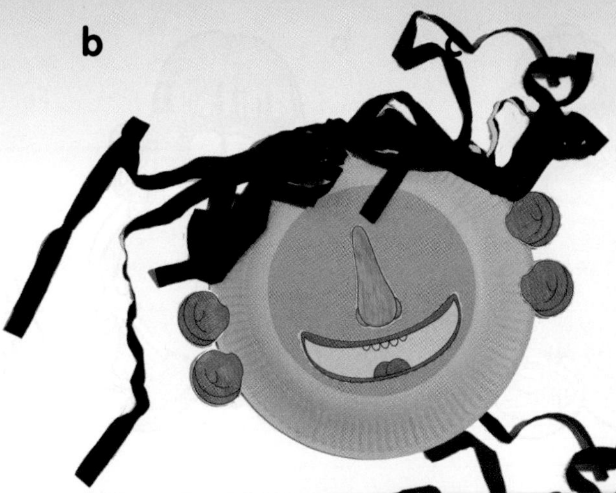

c

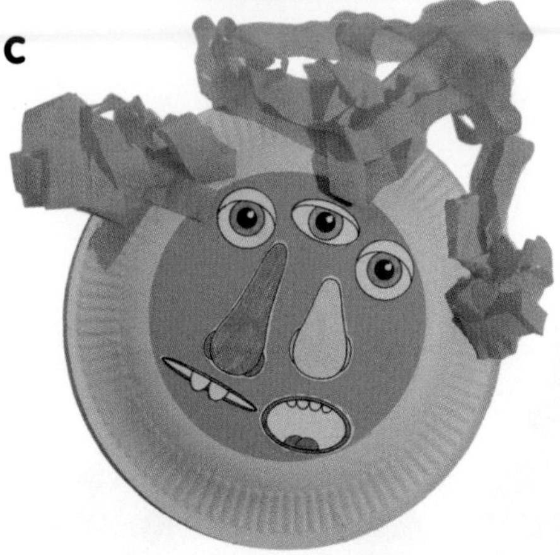

d

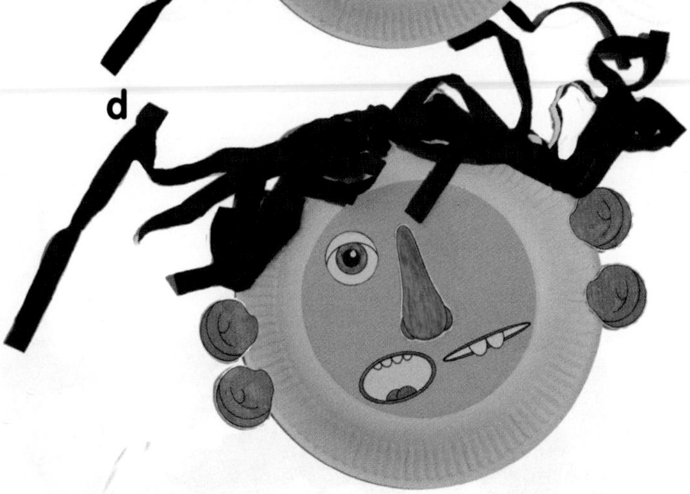

8 Draw and colour. Then say.

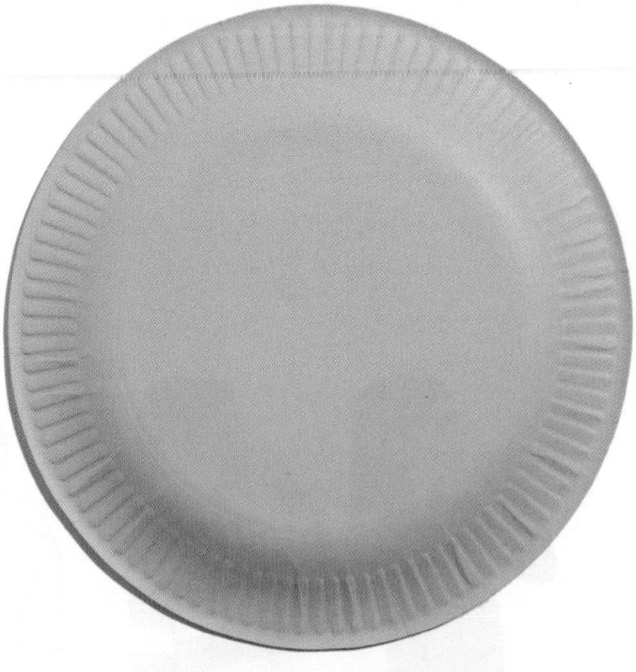

Look! I've got (three eyes) and (two mouths).

9 **Look and say.**

 1
 2
 3
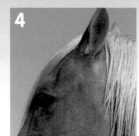 4
 5

10 **Draw and say.**

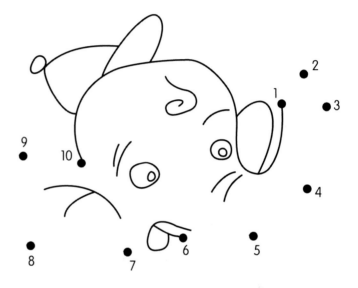

11 **Mime and draw. Then say.**

I can see (an eye).

12 I like salad.

1 Listen and point. Then say. 🔊

2 Look and listen. 🔊

3 Listen again and say. 🔊

ice cream, chips, salad, burger
I like (ice cream). I don't like (salad).

4 Listen and number. •))

a [1]   b [ ]   c [ ]

d [ ]   e [ ]

5 Draw ☺ or ☹. Then say.

6 Play.

I like (burgers). I don't like (chips).
What's this? Ice cream. I like ice cream.

69

Listen and stick. Then sing. •))

8 **Listen and circle.** •))

1

☺ ☹

2

☺ ☹

3

☺ ☹

4

☺ ☹

5

☺ ☹

6

☺ ☹

I like (burgers). I don't like (chips).

9 **Choose and stick. Then say.**

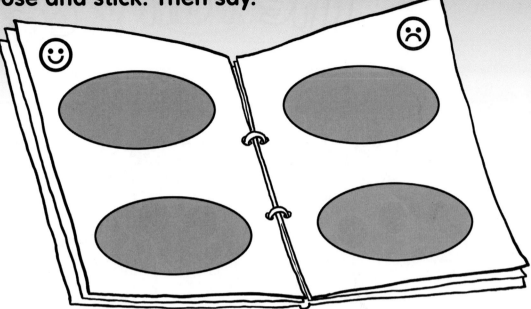

10 **Draw and colour.**

11 **Play.**

I like (bananas). I don't like (pizza).
Salad and chips, please. Thank you.

The fairy café

 Listen and point. Then say. •))   **Look and listen.** •))

dragon, fairy
My favourite!; please; No, thank you.

Act out.

Jungle Fun 6

1 **Stick and say.**

1

2
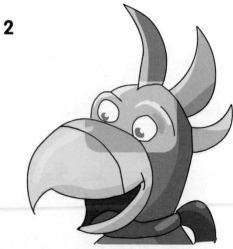

3

4

2 **Draw. Then play.**

3 **Match, draw and colour. Then say.**

4 **Draw and make. Then say.**

I like (cake). I don't like (burgers). My favourite food is (chips).

Happy New Year

1 Listen and point. Then say. 🔊

2 Stick and say.

fireworks, sparkler, calendar

3 Listen and number. Then sing.

4 Colour and make.

Happy New Year! Look at the calendar! Wave your sparkler!

Family Day

1 **Listen and point. Then say.** 🔊

2 **Look and find. Then say.**

family, park
kite, sister, nose, brother, ball, dad, bike, mum

3 **Listen and point. Then sing.** ◀))

4 **Draw and make.**

My Picture Dictionary

1

2

Story Time 1

3

4

     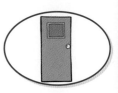

Story Time 2

5

6

Story Time 3

7

8

Story Time 4

9

10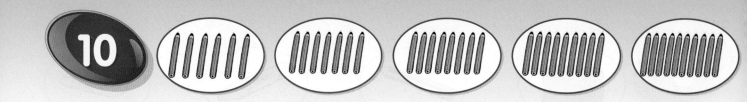

Story Time 5

11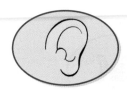

12

Story Time 6

Festival 1

Festival 2

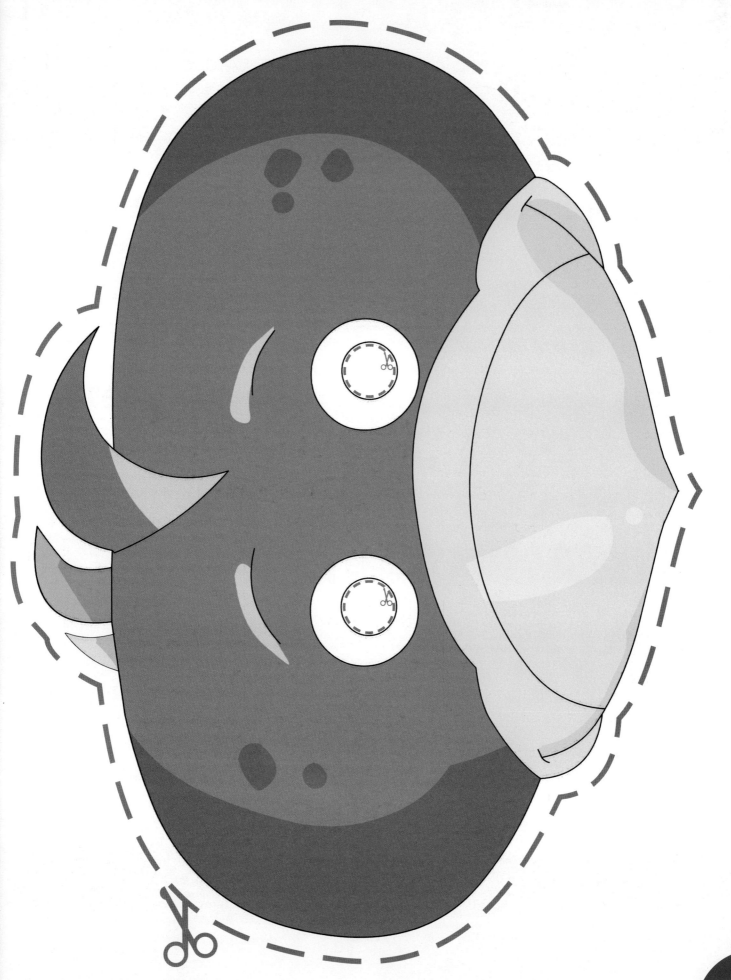